THE FABULOUS RELATIVES

Stephen Smith was born in 1964 in Stourbridge, Worcestershire. He moved to Wales in 1978, living in and around Aberystwyth, and graduated in English from the University College of Wales, Aberystwyth, in 1987. After two years of doctoral research, he worked as a hospital cleaner and life model, and then taught in Japan for a year. He won an Eric Gregory Award for his poetry in 1991. He is now living in Croydon, and teaches Creative Writing at Sutton College of Liberal Arts. *The Fabulous Relatives* is his first collection.

THE FABULOUS RELATIVES

STEPHEN SMITH

Shre Sn.

Jo angrla.

all Th Bt

Shve .

z .

BLOODAXE BOOKS

Copyright © Stephen Smith 1993

ISBN: 1 85224 213 2

First published 1993 by
Bloodaxe Books Ltd,
P.O. Box 1SN,
Newcastle upon Tyne NE99 1SN.

Bloodaxe Books Ltd acknowledges
the financial assistance of Northern Arts.

Cover printing by J. Thomson Colour Printers Ltd, Glasgow.

Printed in Great Britain by
Bell & Bain Ltd, Glasgow, Scotland.

for my grandmothers
Sally Ricketts & Cissy Smith

Acknowledgements

Acknowledgements are due to the editors of the following publications in which some of these poems first appeared: *Aireings, Ambit, Bête Noire, Cyphers, The Echo Room, Envoi, Foolscap, The Honest Ulsterman, London Magazine, Orbis, Outposts, Poetry Nottingham, Scratch, Verse* and *The Wide Skirt*. 'Beside Lough Neagh' was included in *The Forward Book of Poetry 1993*.

Some of these poems were included in a collection for which Stephen Smith received an Eric Gregory Award from the Society of Authors in 1991.

The author is also grateful to Coral Sunman and Douglas Houston for all their support and encouragement, and to Asako Ito for showing him Japan.

Contents

9   Journey in Winter
10 Cold Turkey Pilgrimage
14 The Ringers
15 The Railway Crane
16 Ulster Holiday
17 Hitching
18 Captain Death
19 The Dream of St Cuthbert
20 Tinker, Tailor
21 Original Theatre
22 The Death Shop
23 The Fabulous Relatives
24 On the Exhumation of Seamus Heaney 2220
25 The Caliphs of Hashish
26 Sheffield Park Gardens
27 The Move
28 Letter from Chiba Prefecture
29 Lake Chusenji Letter
30 Bangkok Nights
31 Accident
32 The Mosquito Country
33 January 6
34 Journey with My Son
35 The Fabulous Relatives Speak
36 Him
37 Heterodoxy
38 Rainstorm on the Izu Peninsula
39 The Fly Fisherman
40 The Butterfly Girls
41 The Cortina Boys
42 Between Omagh and Cookstown
43 The House Made of Paper
44 The Dead Stand Up as Trees
45 Danegeld
46 Poor Tom
49 Meat Is Murder
50 Letters to Myself
53 Meeting the Comedians
54 The Twelfth Night Sonnets

56 A Death by Tarmac and Combustion Engine
57 Prison Visit
58 The Execution Shed
59 Introducing Hathaway
60 Hathaway and High Brasil
62 Hathaway and the Dominican Fathers
63 Hathaway's Dialogue
64 Hathaway's Afterlife

Journey in Winter

The black months: December, January –
three hours each side of noon, a brief, limpid
fluorescence. The immediate landscape
squeezed to a pith: long grass and the hollyhocks'
skeletons laid flat in the gardens like old matting.

Better to stay at home; travel only with cause.
The train climbed slowly into the Pennines,
eye registering halts like notches on the curved
blade of track. Wiping the window of steam,
noticing the transits of arrival, departure.

At the end of the line your city and you.
Pointless adolescent speculation
about what you are doing, wearing – the reduction
of love to tangible knowledge. Always
this way: trust petered out. I require a diary

of your week. Easy to fake. Home, I'm exhausted
by pursuing nuances in your speech. Interrogative
silences – a blind game like spying on an enemy's
codes. There will be fewer of these journeys in future
I say as a test. You agree.

Cold Turkey Pilgrimage
(for Coral Sunman)

The real-life slap of what it meant to bottom out hit me.
Before there'd been escape routes planned through others' homes,
my credit good enough to stand a shave
with those who owed me one for fixing deals.
They were places I could relocate, asylums
where I sat to study stations carefully.
Trains intrigued me: I followed tracks across the map
noting connection times. My favoured route was North.
I marked the journeys of the early saints;
they were emblems of sufficient celibacy;
their rigorous catharses were well known.
Some stood for hours under the rivers' lips,
until they owned their motives totally.
I wished to follow them into the solitary.

A friend who used to "jack me up" told me
he had recurring dreams. He would be led
into a hangar large enough to model as the world,
completely dark but full of the quick beat
of pigeons' wings that stirred warm currents on his face.
His guide was always silent but he guessed
his father from the heavy tread and wheeze
of asthma. After some minutes they would stand
beside a pit, which shape he felt from gusts of air.
He had a fear of falling. Always with his legs outstretched
he'd find his depth, treading the water of his crash
with Valium or weights of hash. He had
a fascination though asleep to tuck his arms
beneath his pectorals and fall forever.

I put my faith in anodynes, believing
medieval herbalists who advocated
poison's purgatives as kill or cure.
I went straight on methadone for weeks, exchanging
horror at my need of doing anything
to score, for easy pastures of the prescribed fix.
The hits were pure but lacking genius.
I felt de-scaled, de-toxed, almost clean.
Conversations with psychiatrists did me in,
who accessed to my past and made me puke.
I had to reinvent myself, not only in my head
but put on weight, to recognise myself
in mirrors. I hated them. I only had the clothes to fit
a perfect, junky anorexic.

In hospital with other mendicants
outwardly whole but sick, someone suggested
tales to pass the day along the stations
of our pilgrimage – something to teach
and entertain as Aristotle says.
They came from all quarters of the clock,
from a Methody firebrand whose medicinal
intake caused him to stumble and forget his flock,
to one who would not eat the Sunday Lamb.
She said, 'This is the symbol of the Agnus Dei –
my son.' It so fell out that I was privy
to their private griefs. I recall one whose
heterodoxy was extreme, an army doctor
who'd been with Eisenhower on the Rhine.

He was at the overhaul of Dachau
processing refugees and vaccinating
for typhoid. He had a brutal memory
of dousing pits with chlorine to control
disease. His simple metaphor of skulls
gambolling like potatoes from the fires
chilled me and forced him home to Sunderland.
He practised for a while, his routine punctured
with a patent cocktail from his cabinet.
One spike trailed off the agonies and left
him checking off the dead like football scores.
He was struck off for theft. His story made the Sunday news.
He died while I was there. I wept.
Therapy harrowed him but missed the crime.

Our consumption was totted up at each week's end.
The lowest aggregate would win extended
privileges in the coming days. Sound
methodology of carrot and stick
reduced our private conferences
to snooping at your neighbours' arms.
No one wore T-shirts anymore. The stories too tailed off.
Each concentrated on his own biography.
I fingered pens occasionally
and felt as lonely as Edward Lear,
whose limericks appalled me with their mixture
of the prosaic and the very queer.
He came to visit too wearing a Gladstone hat,
goosing the nurses with a desperate cheer.

At night the even dripping of a tap
mimicked the tread of the atomic clock.
Whole ages passed between each tock
of falling water. By morning I had travelled
through geology's shale locks
from ammonite to homo-ferox.
I felt older than Methuselah –
a survivor of electric shocks.
Doctors took me to pieces and then
assembled something in the shape of man.
Women I had thought had long abandoned me
were gentle then; they bought me books and tangerines.
You the last visitor have stayed almost a year,
your love an antidote to purchases bought dear.

The Ringers

Bohemians existed on the borders of our awareness.
They grew special by denied association –
rough men who called on my Dad selling cars:

'Ringers' in my mother's parlance. For a long time
we considered this a generic expression
for their disturbance at odd hours on our doorbell.

The days after their visits my father would be shut
in his workshop with spray cans, only emerging to eat.
They developed a fabular status akin to Wise Men,

by virtue of the gifts their journeys conveyed to us.
Just as we grew used to trinkets bought with their gold
their midnight arrivals ceased. We decamped shortly

after into Wales and the hush money ended.
Now Dad kept busy with tractors and the odd day's labour
fencing on farms. We were certain of returning in time

to the good life, little princes in exile –
it took years to shrug off our innocent burdens.

The Railway Crane

The stations were all stopped with snow.
Broadcasts listed disrupted services;
sleet flurried to and fro.
I kept a slow communion with sleep,

or talked to porters who passed me,
stamping the ice from off their feet.
Their words were kilted in an Irish brogue.
They shared their bacon and black tea.

I sat while dawn extended a thin gesture
of surprise across the sidings and coal-yard
till you arrived, your gold head folded in a Russian
shawl, your words deciphering delays.

You made your speech diffident and sad. I did not hear.
I watched a railway crane's luminous transformation,
sun limbering slowly up its cabled steel height,
till dangerous as a hawk it balanced on the light.

Ulster Holiday

Hills the night slurred bullied the day,
their dull sinews binding the bay
and all the petty life of eye and soul
inside the prison of a natural bowl.

My relatives kept a summer-house up there
for holidays. Ethnic and three parts bare
it's where they went to practise Gaelic,
to empathise and ape the rural Mick.

Pictures from my album nicely convey
their leisure. Grandad supervising hay
into a cart with business-like concern,
Grandmother spooning tea from a brass urn.

They brought their prejudices up with them,
accumulated from a string of men
with managerial control and skill.
Experienced in Ulster protocol

Grandma kept Fenians on the doorstep
while Grandad paid their cheques.
She saw no reason to condone she said
uppitty values conned from the dead

they venerated in their rebel songs,
and priests talked up in foreign tongues.
Chiefs of the Protestant Ascendency
they liked the feudal order of dependency

on them. The shop of sense was shut
on this issue. Bias descended like the foot
of night. The hills entrenched their view
of Time's gracious penury and nothing new.

Hitching

Many who stopped were lost on the gaunt city's edge:
lorry-drivers ferrying industrial parts
to the wilderness, concrete bulk-heads and huge water fans
to drive electricity out of the rivers.
All needed conversation to humanise long distance
loneliness. They went by arterial highways,
rolling across causeways, spanning jerry-built slums.
Big-eyed children waved us goodbye from bridges.
You can learn a lot about the nature
of pilgrimage from these journeys – direct concentration
converging on a grid point; necessary ignorance
of poverty on route. If you listen to some drivers
dark worlds open out. Between Scotch Corner and Edinburgh
one turned his cab into a confessional,
told how he cheated a wife with young girls in small towns.
Others have missions, one with the handle John 4
browbeat my heterodoxy with quotations from Paul.
You learn tact, the gift of restraining opinions.
Remember the middle-aged man who broke down outside Banbury
about a blind daughter. You thanked him for the lift – 20 miles.

Captain Death

The quiet man next door had bits of war inside him.
It seemed a joke as kids how Dresden's giant pain
could tuck under his belt; how you could put a hat on Dachau.
He frightened us with stories of the Burma Road.

We watched him kill a fox, bare hands snapped its back.
He'd eaten dogs. There was a crazy relish in his grin.
We smirked but went home cold to bed and could not sleep.
He nailed the creature to the hen-house door.

We would follow him in indian-file across the wood,
ducking when he ducked to sidestep dropping shells.
He taught us how to lime small birds
and string them through the throat on nylon thread.

Death's own familiar was a special kind of hero.
We cried the day he hanged himself. He threw his braces
round the hen-house beam and dropped.
Long service medals rolled like pennies round his feet.

The Dream of St Cuthbert

I dreamt the venerable St Cuthbert was alive
seated on a rock in the North Sea,
watching the Russian trawlers through an opera glass
skid on the tide round Scapa Flow.

Questions concerning his longevity were misplaced;
he'd bartered frock and cowl for baccy and new breeches
with a pilot frisked among the bladderwrack.
A cockle-hat he wore askew like Admiral Benbow.

He longed for news of men he said. He tired
of the ventriloquy of skulls he carefully scrubbed
with moss and sand. He thought at last the rough trade
of a woman's jaw might sound like angels quickened by the Host.

I left him winking at the stranger joke of sainthood.
He explained the solitary sexuality of God:
the gorgeous monogamy to which he'd trained
was a cold wife along the arctic nights.

Tinker, Tailor

Tinker, tailor, soldier, sailor,
rich-man, poor-man, beggar-man, priest.

The nursery humour of my cousins ran to bigotry.
They learnt the feudal stations of the artisan –
declined with relish down to priest
from shipwright uncles rich in Harland Wolff.

Elections by Kabbala of the prune stones' plan
were rigged or calculated miscounts.
We dreaded the conviction of the eighth placed man
like Silver's spot unfolded on the fist.

It was the outcast's role, the bogeyman
they kept in check by solemn reverences
made by men, and spells accorded to Melchizedek,
they learnt by rote in arcane convocations

of the Orange Clan. They wielded power
of poverty or fame. They liked it thus.
They made it clear the auguries of fate
excepted us. We were the chosen tribe;

our fetish was correct, till time, demography
or economic entropy might redefine the nursery
code to: tatter, trader, merchant-sailor,
taxed-man, dole-man, beggar-man, thief.

In Bogside households too, perhaps,
are old rhymes remade to arraign
the double-vision of this nations's claims.
Do they express: tinker, tailor, soldier,

sailor, Prot-man, policeman, gunman, grief?

20

Original Theatre

Death makes great theatre. Your burial revived
careers for the prodigal and out of work amongst us.
Licensed to extend our grief beyond the one-act
drama of interment, ours was a show
our self assurances persuaded us could run and run,
to anecdote, private soliloquy and best of all
exaggerated postures: fast ones gulling
a believing audience who gave up rational
enquiry for stall seats at the funeral tea.
We had it all our way, the backdrop guaranteed
a hit. The muscular arrangement of the hills
buoyed up the pastor's voice to a colossal
stentor's pitch. Scene one was glibly done,
anticipated bonhomie would carry us to climax
in scene three. Line perfect till my brother's fumble
at the grave, an unscripted tour-de-force
that pain not innovation made Absurd.
Ours and spectators' horror when he plunged off stage,
his blind walk through the bubble of imaginative control.

The Death Shop

The Death Shop had relocated
to a bright shopping mall. UNDER NEW MANAGEMENT
said a sign picked out in neon. Gaudily
furbished like a souvenir grotto it was doing
brisk trade. A marketing drive to "up-tempo"
image dispensed with old fashioned regalia
at rock bottom prices. Attractive part-exchange
on discontinued lines of memorial urns
was a winner. 'Anything considered' involved
one assistant in off-setting costs
of stabling horses from a Victorian hearse
against synthetic coffins. Sentimental morality
was a no-no. Several far from tubercular
ladies flounced over tills registering cash-sales.
Customers browsed Pic'n'Mix buckets of pills
labelled 'Go for it Sucker'. Speakers played
muzak by Bach. There was something for everyone:
corners devoted to baroque demises,
a D.I.Y. section on kitchen euthanasia.
Really there was too much to see. I said I'd call back.
Management assured me there'd be no need,
already they had teams of trained salesmen
out in the provinces. I could expect a knock soon.

The Fabulous Relatives

My fabulous relatives, all of whom
have jumped throught the hoop of metaphor,
obedient as circus beasts schooled out
of wantonness, your slow collapses
into myth are stopped. For old time's sake

and the cathartic duties owed
an audience, I let you growl.
You were adepts at putting frighteners
on kids but now your trigger idioms
are tamed. Your malice serves my sweet

phraseology. All of you named
Union patriots or simply clowns
accede to burlesque tricks of vaudeville:
butt ends of humour, my sad fall guys
dance antics to my whipping pen.

On the Exhumation of Seamus Heaney 2220

Visceral investigations revealed
important aspects of his diet. Seed gruel
showed he was careful of cholesterol.
Several Martian scientists

argued certain stains upon his fingers
were vegetable extracts compatible with ink.
He was a possible disseminator
of knowledge to an age before telepathy.

Learned treatments were called for, extending
sympathies between these physiological
discoveries; conjecture catalogued
him in the end as having been

an agronomist, whose portfolio
was educational instruction of the mass.
Mildewed papers, his illegible grave-goods
found buried with him settled this.

The Caliphs of Hashish

I met the Caliphs of Hashish in the Old Alhambra's
back-bar, where they drank all day after time.
A proficiency in the language of need bolstered
by hard cash was necessary to enter.
Their room smelt of grass and metal heated too long on the stove:
knives for slicing the hash into weights. Etiquette
had to be followed: you watched your step, taking your cue
from the Main-Man's laugh. Careful not to leave too soon you sat
hearing the rap about hot-goods. Never straight
in their company, my history grew fabulous,
night time raids on allotments to eke out the dole
assumed the bravura of military tactics.
Their nods were indulgent, licence to go on,
ceding me amateur status. Habitual use
made them dangerous as children who lived in a land
where frogs were capable of princedom and you could shatter
a man's legs with legitimate violence.

Sheffield Park Gardens

Five months to Pentecost
and the efflorescence of St Elmo's fire
charging the ground with blue darts of crocuses.
January tastes of morphine and dull dreams,

an emaciate season when notional
salvators are mislaid. Gone out from my country
where the dead are interred under palanquins
of flowers into a county of iron,

where the drill slips on wet granite and sheers
shallow graves in the Municipal Cemetery.
Come with a lover to try virtues of an old
allegiance, the last time for a career

of cold beds and misunderstandings. No good.
Fastened to first pain, learning the hard way
that even the bride is only paroled
by the grave. Everything bitched.

The Move

The morning light glistened like Blue-John slag
over Sheffield, polishing the birch trees
to the lustre of chrome. The flat was dizzy
with brightness. On TV a test match

was starting; sun through the curtains caught
the bowler's first ball in flight and dissolved it
in atoms. In whites, the cricketers
were slimmed to a ghostly translucency.

You moved round the rooms, stuffing various
costumes into black plastic sacks
you'd earmarked for charity.
This was the bargain you'd struck with a chastity

of sorts, not to recognise yourself
in any more disguises. Your father
was calling at twelve in a van to carry
you back into Wales. A civilised end.

When you'd gone with your boxes and paintings,
I let out the cat, hoping it would stray,
then went back inside to the cricket.
Later I could think imagination had lost you.

Letter from Chiba Prefecture
(for Douglas Houston)

October 1st. Three weeks gone from Britain.
Distance has lengthened out the days between;
the heat abets a false perspective too
on winter climbing through its gears of cold,
salting the trees with ice outside your window.
Here sun is hot and I have Maugham for guide:
he dribbles gin and plays the old colonial to me.
His talk is crude and anecdotal; his native
parodies insouciant. He shambles
in his slippers and house-coat around the flat,
camping it up with other exiles given
leave to loom out of my head.

Auden is here, complaining of the food
and Thai-Boys that he had in China.
He asks me how I keep my two rooms clean
in a nicely modulated alexandrine.
Lawrence (T.E.) is keen to solve the mystery
of why he skipped and missed the War and try out bikes.
Waugh (no pun intended by the way)
has come out strongly in my sympathy.
I think the lesson of his ship-board ghosts,
whispering inside the air-conditioning
has taught common civility to him.
He always says sorry when he barges in.

These are the principals of my confederacy.
They take delight in pointing out their commonwealth
with me, for noticing those differences from home,
though all of us left to beat ennui.
It's curious how the mind will run: I wonder what
John Donne would have made of the mosquito
not 'The Flea'. D.H. made it the subject
of a nice conceit on usury.
This dressing of the occident in Eastern garb
returns me neatly to T.E. who said,
'Watch your white-skinned morality, lest you like me
misplace your own identity.' His words showed he was out of touch.
Outside my room, Tokyo twitches like a splendid
fish, swallowing the bait of Englishness.

Lake Chusenji Letter

Looking back, the lake was a cold mirror
no one could look in. Ice repelled our
reflections. We were too small even for shadows –
smudged by the long bulk of mountains skidding

their casts over the surface. Below we
watched goldfish breathing water. I think
it's appropriate we could find nothing
of ourselves in that country we leased for a year.

Letters from you remind me of those fish –
you are visible in your calligraphy
but untouchable. You distort in
the distance between us. Beautiful

certainly but time warps our awareness
of each other. We do not even have
our days running in tandem. I set out
for you but light buckles on my journey

before I'm half way; conversations depend
on cables of sound looping the globe.
The first image is the true one. We had no
marker, even together we threw no reflection.

Bangkok Nights
(for Steve Holloway)

Friable days crumble into night.
Clouds topple westwards burnt the colour
of cinders where the city infuses
their basements with neon. Gimcrack signs

flash grottos of lust: The Lotus Motel,
Miss Saigon's Delights. Pederasts advert
special needs in the low parlour door-
ways – anything goes. A young man

with beautiful fingernails will turn
tricks in the cellar of a disused
silk factory, where catalogues
for Yokohama cloth litter the floor.

'Anytime, anyplace, anywhere –
she's the right thing' a pimp squeaks
on the corner. A night wind from the harbour
is just cool enough to excite desire.

Foreigners with dollars tool through the streets.
They are watched for like goldfish in tanks;
language is directed at them: business-
men to seed the East with new products.

Accident
(for Albert Camus)

Landscapes flung away from the eye
equal and drab in the drizzle:

boned by dead contours
the land's in retreat.

Black rain and billboards
hawking hotels on route to the South;

petty villages bleak nor betraying
any regional features ignored,

till time braked and day tautened
to a motif of flat steel and violence

piling invisible taboos against you.
Tyres shrieked on the road sticky with dew

pressing you hard against glass.

Time snapped and made you a stranger
a crown of hours broke with your head.

The Mosquito Country

For twelve hours it has rained without variation,
a heavy warm flood. First sun makes the street giddy
with steam, wavers the contours of buildings to liquid.
The mosquito understands this floating world best,
is a native inured to water-born sickness.
We sweat under netting and dream like opium
eaters poisoned by small incisions in the skin.
The mosquito transmits his knowledge to us,
returns us to primary sensations, fevers
of heat, torpors of cold.
                              For three days I became
the mosquito: saw a land swivel under my eyes.
I fed off its body with greedy insistence,
digested the blood of small-traders loading fruit
on the water-fronts, tasted the plumpness of commerce
in their veins; bit into warrior and Emperor;
was sick on the slack blood of vegetarian
priests; sucked at the nipples of geishas. I was tight
with the sweetness of life. I squatted on their backs
till they grew thin with my drinking, feverish
with my unfamiliar contagions.

January 6

Along with your short body
your long history into that grave
is dropped. We gather in the horizontal rain
a line of ghosts – and relatives
who came as far as office hours allowed –
to pitch domestic trinkets
to the ground with you.
Each one with his gift is partisan:
a Lux flake from a working Mam
who scrubbed for you; a pair of stockings
from the spectre of an overseas GI;
a winkle shell from Galway
and a thimbleful of rusty blood
syringed upon the clay
are tribute from a long dead son;
a rowan berry from a lost
rear-gunner tangled in the masts
of search-lights reared above Berlin,
and last from me, prodigal grandson
of your daughter's blood, a gift
of fingernails and hair.
May they too grow with you beneath the dirt.

B

Journey with My Son

Flat lands. The impression of driving across a map.
On both sides of the road irrigation-ditches sprint
in straight lines to the sea. A horizontal world,
where everything tends to a fixed line of dyke
holding the sky in check. No place for longing
or imagination. The small boy beside me
has agreed to this journey. He is the end
of my reponsibility. I am afraid
of his singular, honest loneliness. An hour
since we made uneasy conversation
about model aeroplanes. Both of us are looking
for excuses for being here.
                          We arrive suddenly,
a deserted airbase. I think this is Hell,
as remote as you get, near the top of the world,
where the Arctic retreats on a concessionary
basis three months a year. Thirty years since the Milwaukee
Airwing flew back to Stateside. Only their graffiti
remain on the Nissen huts' walls. For forty-five
minutes, we toss balsa Spitfires on wires in the wind,
then go back to the car because it is cold.
He looks at me funny. Way back we are buzzed
by a jet – a rip-boom slices the sky.
Too much to be taken on trust, he suffers me.

The Fabulous Relatives Speak

Those ghosts I'd flayed of their bodies came last night.
Those I had changed from wearers of motley
to my own paradigms, stood in my head

like unsummoned Jacks from their boxes. They called
to account disregard for their deaths on my part.
I dreamt that I was Dante Alighieri

with an uncle for a guide across the nightmare ground.
He reckoned up the bodies I'd delayed
in purgatory by relation of their sins,

proved how the half-joke tilted for a laugh in pubs
was instrumental in their pain. I had escaped
into a land where thoughts were engines of despair.

He did not speak. He seemed content to lead.
I did not know I had so many dead,
engaged in all the habits of my tarot

reading of their lives. My mother's mother's
hands showed their stigmata, how they bled
perpetually delivering her still-born son.

She was the emblem I had made for prolix grief.
Beside her knelt my cousin Mick painting Cromwell
with his toes. His task was a perspective

warts and all. I cried that I had seen enough.
I woke to sunbeams falling in a stream
of fishscales on the street.

Him

(for Roy Ricketts, d. 1980)

Sometimes I still mistake you labouring
uphill to meet me, both lungs wheezily
using too little air; your half a heart
closing your pace to a shuffle at the top –

only a game my conscience plays with me.
Your last years shrank you to a pygmy
in another man's clothes, incapable
of a short walk to the toilet. Catheters

eased your necessity but made you cry
like a child. By now water's attrition
will have scaled you down further to reducible
proteins mixed with the dirt. Our relation

to each other has not healed though ten years'
space is between us. Murders on a small-
scale, what families are best at tangled
our respect for each other, making filial

emotions unnatural. They took me to visit
you at the end. It would have been easy
not to recognise love, stayed at the door
ashamed by your death. You played with my finger

while I sat by your side, conversation
beyond you. I've hated your going a decade,
would have liked your opinions, might have liked
you to stop me taking liberties with the dead.

Heterodoxy

My piscivorous auntie who ate white flesh on Fridays,
for whom worship was an art of refinement
that began on the palate and ended in manners
had a wholly new theology centred on meat.

Some claimed her mad, recalling how she meditated
Herod's slaughter of the babes in the infant
blush of veal, or how she eyed the chicken's corpse
in hope of the miraculous, in case it should

sit up and crow, 'Christus natus est' as in legend
it was wont to do. Beef with its memory of the blood
still in the gravy proved a totem too
of what the bitter thorns had done. Admittedly,

it was a private fetish that lent this sanctity
to meat. Uninterested in the orthodox
she made her stations to the Godhead in the roast,
serving wafer slivers in deference to the Host.

Rainstorm on the Izu Peninsula

Black oblong rain camouflaged the sun;
figures took cover with delayed slow-
motion hesitancy – wind stunned. Sound

thickened to a dull rasp of rain pellets
hitting the road. Insects zipped in the air
twitching skin with their small feet.

Sensitive to time read off in millionths
they swerved through the drops, like flying
between a downpour of telegraph poles.

World was enormous seen through their eyes.
Words filtered by satellite across oceans
bring me no closer to you.

Weather news and gossip try to duplicate love.
The cold rain falling mimics long dashes
of morse, me calling you, unable to be honest.

The Fly Fisherman
(for Jack Mason)

There was something deliberate and slow like the process of digestion
in the way his fingers worked, paring the feathers with a scalpel
      blade –
a microscopic wit in how he made the callous hook a mimic for the
      trout's affection.
His was an artistry conceived among minutiae.
When he was dead I thought of irony that tied the cancer in his gut
and played him on a line of nerves, of how perspectives altered;
of how his fear swam to the surface on a hook.

The Butterfly Girls

The cities are at war with boredom;
twilight's fractured with neon and klaxons.
Local idols crawl round the squares
in souped-up Cortinas painted
with Confederate flags. Girls in butter-
fly skirts preen under beansticks on the Council
allotments for them. Being cool
is paramount: the boys pretend to be
Jean-Paul Belmondo and the girls masticate
gum like Bardot. Anthems crash from the stereos,
songs about teen-love and tragedy.
Migrations towards heaven are arranged
behind factories, where rings and CDs are bartered
for closeness. Emotion's on HP.
When they've gone the square's empty except
for their aerosol signatures on walls.
Half of them I can't read.

The Cortina Boys
(for Jock McFadyen)

The Cortina Boys are switched onto speed.
A hundred mph rocks the clock, puts
the landscape in traction. They drag round the block,
windows lazily down, injecting the late
summer breeze with their spleen. They play White Blues
on the radio and hum songs about
the Confederate Dead, fragrant in the smashed
gardens after Bull Run. They drawl in a language
exclusive to them; they defend territories
their minds have imagined: a mile and a half run
from Streatham to Norbury. There, they hang ugly
banners on the walls, challenging Niggers
to work or go home. To be a brother
you can't be black and must be the right sort
of white. They are clannish. 'The White Knights'
blazoned on their "bombers" parodies chivalry.
They imagine themselves back to the wide
Mississippi, dressed in fine cotton suits, peonies
in their hands, walking through a gauze of water sprinklers,
employing black maids for Missy.

Between Omagh and Cookstown

Between Omagh and Cookstown a waiting place:
the road going straight through peat fields and ditches,
from ground or air, a scenery chosen for brochures.

Remains on the burnt verges: snap-bags, thermoses, dentures.
We arrive guided by policemen and film-crews.
It's a struggle to say anything new or shocking –

fact goes off at a tangent into myth,
language stakes claims. Drizzle turns to ice on the tarmac,
making movement circumspect, hesitant.

Later in sleep I return unhindered by check-points.
The moon has expanded in the sky, creasing
perspective under its ambiguous lamp.

Workmen are thinned to spindly shadows in its half day.
I am more moved in my dream than reality.
The moon rescues the territory for its cold, dead self.

The House Made of Paper

Even today it needs a fantastic journey to reach you.
I see the eight time zones driven into the map, a succession of
girders splicing the diurnal. You will be sitting
in your house made of paper, a kimono bandaging your nakedness.
The flared neon fluorescence of clip-joints and amusement arcades
in Kabuki-Chuo tattooing your neck with semi-precious stones.
Around you night breathes a confectionery of unguents.
In the distance the clatter of trams and a wolf's yap
in the Zoo filter through the *shojii*. You'll be fixing your hair
for the evening, wearing the ugliness of the geisha's pallid
emulsion. On the table before you broad brushes for rouge
and the stubbed out crayon of a lip-gloss.
I don't like your life, your assumption of gratefulness for kisses.
Too far to reach and my prerogatives run out like a tourist's.
I am in a house with a large view of trees at autumn's beginning.
I want you to stay still in your house made of paper, or a great
wind to blow in the doors: great acres of snow in your lap.

The Dead Stand Up Straight as Trees

(The Seamen's Cemetery, Hachijojima Island)

The dead stand up straight as trees
against a land culled of redundant gestures.
Humanity's action is minimal,
the one-storyed village backs off from the sea.

Corridors of the dead file purposely
the frayed edges of history
to a sharp definition. Here
faith is cruel, outlandish fidelity

insisted on. Figures curious in piety
shuffle against the wind's authority
bunches of grass into bouquets,
scarce worship of the gone.

Love as meaning has none.
The sea leaches emotion away from their beds.
Ritual's awful mendacity
is a static, unrewarded credit.

Heaven is empty above, debiting
their sorry, closed accounts further.
Before a flat architecture of burnt
rocks, the sea edits life's coming and going.

Danegeld

I saw North derelict: counties abandoned to rain,
the towns left to investigation by wolves,
factories beached by the longshore drift of money South.
Migrants appeared on our borders, men with strange accents.
Reports said the crossroads were blocked.
We waited their visit, trussing accounts of our learning
into sacks. We slept scarcely,
and then dreamt of precedent endings: Rome's collapse
into squalor, camp fires lit with our churches.
Bargains must have been struck at the top,
a Danegeld paid. The Barbarians never arrived.
Now we have cultural exchanges with them.
We teach in their schools and they show us new
ways to trim gold in elaborate patterns.
The current vogue is to give children their names,
a fetish believing they will not slay their own.

Poor Tom

Poor Tom at Vukovar

I saw Poor Tom completely mad
on peak-time TV live last night
from Vukovar. Straight from Baghdad
the BBC's reporter questioned him

inside a church that was shelled-out;
asked for his personal response to rout.
Even a dubbed translation could not close
the obvious distress war had exposed.

His mind refused to recognise landscapes
shelling had sluiced to new contours.
He talked wildly of rape,
torture and grief, aerial spores

that settled on the city through the day.
All his metaphors jumbled and crazy,
the cameraman panned sideways and away
to a shot of smoke drifting hazily.

Listening to Tom

In my head he continued constructing
alibis out of necessity,
his fol-de-rol nonsense surviving
my interference asking Pity.

In the end I allowed his epiphany.
Out of his mouth the dead emerged singing –
fed on war's gluttony.
I heard a baby's cot song and mothers keening.

He poured hell in my ears. Through his vision
I entered a place of terrible progeny,
which language could never inform on,
where words made no sensible advocacy

of anything. Politics, love, sex and defeat
all such thoughts were returned to the nursery.
This was madness not a cheat –
lullay, lullay, a ballad of lunacy.

Poor Bastard Tom

Poor Tom had slain deliberately
his unchosen ancestry,
wearing madness's cloak of motley
to advertise his bastardy.

This kept him safe from claims
and counter claims about fraternity.
Whole villages were numbed and put to sleep
by gun's insistence on egality.

It seemed the whole world had turned to homicide.
Neither tribe would take him in.
He took war's tundra as his bride –
walking sadhu-like to slough off sin,

through land subsiding into graves.
His songs passed understanding now,
their frozen, celibate ravings
incapable of asking why or how.

Recognition will not come this time
morticing morality to tragedy
at the end. No sweet solution to rhyme
versuses to a patched harmony,

to meld collapse of age and tyranny
to a kinder kingdom's hope.
Snow falls like a curtain at the end
on Tom with a white hush like dope.

I still see Tom, meddling with crazy
tunes, still whimpering, 'Poor Tom's a cold.'
No one now translates what he says.
He walks across a map treaties have sold.

Exit to a fanfare of jets.
The country buckles under their gaze.
Tom will continue to mince and to fret,
his mad song dispersed in their rage.

Meat Is Murder

On the abattoir wall someone has sprayed
the unequivocal MEAT IS MURDER.
I linger for a smoke and test
the evident Brahmin's dislike of steak,
beside the irony of the sacred cow
wallowing in the truck of human waste
in Delhi's broiling stews.
Debate seems viable; I recall that phrase
in Forster's most eclectic book,
concerning whether wasps have souls;
the quite unliterary protests of my youth
spent in a Midland town occur,
where John Bull reared his head
calling the local halal house unclean.
I've visions of the Empire as a carnivore
devouring half the globe.
A history of meat is not absurd.
I have a scam for burlesques
on the protein's role in cannibal society.
Satire is abrupted though and horror real
when through the concrete wall I hear
the cattle's plunge and human squeals:
the noise the drowned make under water.

Letters to Myself

I

A long time now since I've been *home*,
keeping abreast of news as best I can:
writing letters or talking down the phone
to relatives who've stood their ground

on the Shankhill side of the Green Line.
The family's organic sense splintered
since my mother's side decamped across
the water to the Forties War;

eroded further by elimination rounds:
disease and quarrels spawned by wills.
A feeling that they humour my naivety –
I'm caught offside by their reality

of living daily in the gun's clean sight.
I have evolved a Popish heresy,
my sympathies half faith, half irony
are taken as a gospel flagrancy

by aunts who'd leave the room if I played
Kevin Barry on the stereo. My English
vowels are all wrong; my anecdotes would be exposed
by going home. If I went back I'd be a tourist.

II

I'm uncertain where my bias lies,
which is my country, this domicile
where I draw dole or that other
frequently patrolled in dream.

I'm going back to make reports:
postcards or airmail bulletins
returned to sender at my home address –
attempts to argue with myself.

III *A Postcard from Finvoy Street*

I was brought here in nineteen seventy
in my first suit, to be obedient
to a relic of mortality.

The house was packed. I slept upstairs
between grandparents in the room
above the parlour where the body lay.

Loss was communicated to me
by the flowers' odour and a tang
of bleaching fluids in the house.

The furniture was scrubbed each day
to eradicate the germ of death.
Quiet looped like a noose throughout

the house. The body lay in state, dressed
like Caruso, an orange cummerbund
hiding its paunch, a bowler hat across

its chest. My mother kissed its grinning
lips. I tasted cold and made a fuss.
Its smirk grew wider as I cried.

Those days had a pantomime quality.
I feel now for his wife whose grief was lost
inside the crude hyperbole

of burying that hero of his Lodge.
Dead, he still seemed capable of anything
like getting up and taking tea with us.

Twenty years have modified my childish fear
but still he looms enormously behind me.
If I had a stake, I'd drive it through his heart.

IV *Beside Lough Neagh*

The lough's peaty intestines throw back
no mirror image of the sky.
The lough's dark centre sucks the sunlight
in like a black star. Here my fathers

worked the linen crops in '17,
weaving khaki blankets for the troops,
till flax-lung bandaged up their breath.
The climate's perfect with its yeasty air

for moistening the brittle cloth.
As kids we used to dive in there.
Now I think Sodom and Gomorrah
could be sunk under its depths –

a localised apocalypse,
rating small mention in the world at large.
I imagined Belfast going down on fire.
Here, water's a secret metaphor:

Priests sign a symbol on your head
at birth. Transparent and indelible,
it still feels chilly on my brow;
water washes free the gunman's tracks

from earth. Though Belfast's sunk beneath
its weight, there are mariners
under my blood, who surface now and then
to breathe. They push my accent into grief.

Meeting the Comedians

Another strange meeting, this time in the fissures
of an earthquake country. In my head a traffic-
jam of hearses going round on a carousel.
My companions had the gleefulness of migrants,

the crazed, booming laughs of Hamlet's tragic technicians
performing an unwitting anarchy on the State.
Were they really that dumb, saturating the air
with their knockabout satire? It is difficult

not to laugh at their unsubtle mime. Reflex
jocularity made Ophelia snigger
and loosed Hamlet mad through a stand-up routine
of working men's puns. Out of tragedy's belly

my familiars have come, greaved with an armour
of laughter. Mechanics of deranged, side-splitting
mirth, their eyes are twisted on ludicrousness
and their children are eloquent clowns claiming

jests back from the horror of putsches. They remind
me of Chaplin who made distress eagerly funny.
Friends pushed from bridges or shot, swing through arcs of grand
slapstick. Here in a field they rehearse like a circus,

gild their faces with white masks. Morality is dead;
comedy set free to expose
the connivance of my pity in their heartbreak.
With no maps left to inhabit they dance and clap wildly.

The Twelfth Night Sonnets

About suffering he was clearly wrong.
I listened while he leaned with open arms
across the pulpit, extemporising
on 'The Small Apocalypse' of Mark,
extending his black shadow high above
our heads. He had a vast artillery
of words and a fine tone, delivering
consolation. He talked of Faith and Works,
and how he'd been impressed and moved by her.
He brought to bear the history of two
thousand years in convocation to this
little death, rolled underground with martyrs,
evil men and common dead. A super-
salesman, he almost sold me joy.

Outside Twelfth Night assembled natural
fallacies, the weather geared to a slow,
ponderous interment of the box, slid
on rollers through the mud. We had to shove.
We followed the Pastor up the dirty street
through winter's stripped-down, forcible
language: trees shorn of shade climbing
in straight lines to the mountain grave.
Wind broke westwards off the sea
and dashed his surplice in his face;
dirt smeared the hem of his long coat.
Insignificant details cancelled
by grief then, return to mar
the memory of your going.

March refreshed the axles of the trees
with green. I met the Pastor in the park,
who still had time for homilies
about how Christ had claimed us from the dark.
I envied him his certain faith,
his surety the Lamb would stand his bail
because He'd suffered half a day upon
The Cross. You died for eighteen months,
your body squeezed through morphine dreams
completely out of shape. I wish I could believe.
I can't. There is no easy synthesis
between His love and our pain. I give no heed
to gentleness in any dealings with my God.
He shrives in anger. I ask, 'Where is Love?'

A Death by Tarmac and Combustion Engine

A death by tarmac and combustion engine
caught us by the legs and dropped us in a land
where petty domestics over family rights
were magnified a thousand times in every house.

I thought it was magic how locals could tell
as if by smell the contents of another's
soul. At times I thought that there must be
an invisible shell, each man carried like a snail

upon his back. This was half correct in terms
of metaphor, each man dragged his party
territory round with him. I cottoned on.
Worse, were the visions I saw after learning

this. I found that I could see each one's doorplate
hinged on their face but subtly changed. I counted
them off like epitaphs: this one a Catholic
baker from the Falls, that other a Prot cabbie

from up Newtownards. I saw them changing
into stones that waited to be sunk in good,
brown peat. This was a landscape buckled by hate.
Tunnels excavated by the dead beneath their feet

swayed both sides crooked. In between a deep
subsidence yawned. Like something out of Bosch
a further vision gaped. I saw the old
and not so old descend headlong, some grasping

muskets, others Bibles and broadswords down
into Hell, and while they fell, they babbled
in outlandish tongues, only intelligible
to them about maps and counties green with verdigris.

Prison Visit

The treadmill wheel has left the transfer
of a giant ammonite on the work-
shop wall which rain brings out.
The Governor who's liberal informs
us how his men deploy their stretch
more usefully than then, by going out
and building walls on Council schemes.
He sees his irony and cracks a joke.

Something of the solid Calvinists
who built this place from private means
has passed into the stone. The wings
and prison-yards are tight with checked
hysteria – you can almost smell it.
Human statements: simple love,
small acts of charity are difficult
emotions to express in here;
weakness is assumed a sin.

We pass the ammonite again
on our way out. Its every revolution
desiccated hours and drove iron motors
to explode geology for granite
basins to canals. A harsh exemplum
of doing time. Faith bends away from work;
you're either saved or else you ain't.

The Execution Shed

The execution shed's 20 x 10
of unadorned scrubbed boards was built outside
B Wing; a covered annexe led the way
from the 'queer' cell which time was recessed from.
No warders were allowed to wear a watch,
a humane gesture beaten by the choice
of the word 'shed'. I looked it up; it means
outbuilding set aside from common use,
a place for beasts or implements. Language
so useful as a gloss to monitor
emotion, consecrated these bare feet.
Its primitive hygiene was like a Non-
Conformist Hut, stripped to the minimal
required for their tight ceremony.
I thought about the draughty flitching shed,
cut through by wind in Armagh, where my mother's
Da skimmed the carcasses of pigs with a wet
knife. Memories of that horror were high camp
compared to this. It is almost wicked
to research by words the final history
of this box-room. There are places that syntaxes
can't close, or conversely unlock;
where bodies devolve back before the soul;
when everything is ornamental
but the movements of the gut and a dead smell.

Introducing Hathaway

He sat down beside me on the bus,
introducing himself as a guest
I'd forgotten from a wedding several years previous.
I discovered we had plenty in common
including adjacent addresses.
Next lunch-time a postcard arrived:
a Rousseau reproduction of a bourgeois
with tigers. It suggested he call.

He became a frequent visitor,
dropping in on his way to the library,
where he sat in a carrel till lights out
researching the camouflage of flowers.
He was ex-military
which had lent him an interest in secrecy.
I began to understand he was out of control
the night he turned up wasted on hash
and related his story to a girlfriend of mine.
He frightened her silly.

Next morning he brought in the milk and said sorry,
leaving a copy of Burton's *Melancholy*
with the mail. Whenever he had risked his integrity
he left gifts: books, birds' eggs, foreign stamps.
I tried to excuse him to myself and my friends –
truth was I needed to feel good about letting him belong.

Hathaway and High Brasil

Where the breakwater splits the infinitive
of sea and estuary, Hathaway stumbles
as though he has infected feet. Brought here
along his own itinerary of grief,
he seems to watch his image's miraculous
sea-change amongst the surf.

                Next I see him
underneath the Pier, checking behind the iron
stanchions with his eye, almost like playing
Hide and Seek with someone who's invisible.
He looks up conscious of my scrutiny
and mimes a gesture out to sea.
I try to guess his crude charade but fail
and mime my wrong guess back by semaphore.

He climbs up to me on the road, his breath
rancid with sherry fumes. He talks fast, unique
metaphors that sketch a gorgeous hinterland,
imagined like John Mandeville's key-shaped
peninsula, swarming with fictions of geography.
He's not looking for himself at all,
rather his father who had been First Mate
on HMS *Tempestuous* in '41.
He has his father's log which he takes out and reads.
His voice goes deeper here: the groggy
accents of a strange soliloquy
as if his father works him by ventriloquy.

'Ultima Thule, a place of krakens and ice-floes...
the sea has turned to violet...steer for High Brasil...
we're holed; we're holed...the radio controller dead
at Scapa Flow...we can't raise Septimus
the pilot at Brindisi...'
I couldn't follow these elisions, his father's
interchange with history.

I left him watching the Spring Equinox
pour gales through its mad sluice.
The wrongs of his conviction ceased to worry me.
My own belief in fathers had been equally absurd.
There was something crazed and lonely in his vigilance
but the probity of his emotion frightened me.

Hathaway and the Dominican Fathers

He plotted a map of dementia to spread before shrinks;
learnt a lexicon of medical jargon describing
psychosis to con them. His attempts to get sectioned failed.
Instead, he tried the Church's patronage
of Holy Fools, arriving smashed but penitent
on the local pastor's porch. The housekeeper gave him milk.
He was siphoned off outside the parish.
A kind priest drove him down to Kent, in a big red Volvo
stacked with books. The Gracious Order of Dominicans took him.
They cashed his dole-cheque every second week and dripped
       him money
for an ounce of shag on each fourth day.
Letters he sent from there reminded me of Ivor Gurney;
he described nature's republic that he'd found.
It seemed his life was coming straight when his letters stopped.
I thought perhaps he'd taken the Novitiate.
I wanted this. In my best dreams I saw him quietly
serving Mass and working in the fields. In my worst
I saw him on the road for getting drunk, squabbling
for wine, his Penguin copy of Akhmatova tucked inside his shirt.

Hathaway's Dialogue

Hashish's perfume greased Hathaway's street:
vicious and lonely recreations played out there
behind the dark. I saw him in the spring
when cherry trees were loosing canopies of ash
like thick asbestos on the concrete lots
for knackered cars. He served me green tea in his room –
a period when he was scrubbing clean
with regular syringes of free methadone.
He gave his life away piecemeal in memories
uttered in sardonic dialect:
his mating with another's tongue designed
to distance and make strange the crude emotion
that he owned. His childhood on the Dyfed fens,
when rain alliterated days on end
had introduced him to his father's bent for indoor games.
This was the hard species of love he struggled with.
What frightened him he said, was that each morning
in the mirror, he was brought up close as conversation
with his father's self and similar desires.

Hathaway's Afterlife

The mad and the dead have no right of habeas corpus.
Hathaway irons his bed-sheets and leaves the Mission
for Land Damaged Sailors, through a crack where the brick-
work's fatigued. Outside it is raining and the malls
are walked out on by lovers who've recessed for winter.
Hathaway's actions are now circumstantial,
something is missing like an amputee's legs
that still burn their sinews in his brain. A loss
he balanced out before by filching coins
from passing trade, to stun himself against the cold
and whatever happened next or didn't.
The city twitches like aquarium fish
behind the rain and echoes with anaemic voices
that recall, questions requiring answers mouthed
by Davy Jones, that circulate under the Gulf
Stream to the coast of Wales from Mexico.
Hathaway watches Friday evening usurers
who offer interest on love to wives at home,
negotiate immediate pay-offs to girls
who're quitting clubs. Hathaway is uninvented
by this kind of love; he gets his kicks from periscopes
in lavatories. His love is contraband and bad.
Hathaway's afterlife refuses change.
He smiles unaware that he's dead and the city
inherited by dog-foxes' cries. At the moment
of eloquence his words emerge dumb. He leaves off
going nowhere, a sequence of non-developed
dates congeal in his head and judgement's deferred.